Francesca

By SARAH H. BARNARD

Illustrated by Katherine Bourdon
Applewood Press
MMXVI

Copyright © 2016 by Sarah H Barnard
Published by Applewood Press, Muskegon, MI 49441
All rights reserved.
This is a work of fiction. Names, characters, places and incidents either are the product of the author's imagination or are used fictitiously, and any resemblance to any actual persons, living or dead, events, or locales is entirely coincidental.

No part of this publication may be reproduced, or stored in a retrieval system, or transmitted in any form or by any means, electronic mechanical, photocopying, recording or otherwise, without written permission of the publisher.

ISBN: **0997959304**
ISBN-13: **978-0997959307**

Printed in the U.S.A.
First Edition, 2016

FOR JACOB & SALLY

This one's for you, Mom and Dad,
whose unconditional love and encouragement
provided a comfortable base for discovering and spreading my wings.
Big bear hugs up to you both! ♥

Special Acknowledgements
Thank you: Annie Sheppard, Laura Hayes, Josh Bourdon, Diane Walkowski, Elizabeth Prentice, Steve Barnard and Craig Bourdon

In her own little world,

a home beautiful and sound,

There sat a spoiled pup

on a soft, puffy mound.

Her name was

Francesca

and as one might guess

Her looks were astonishing;

yet her thoughts

... quite a mess.

Her soft, beautiful fur

was pristine and luxurious -

Silky brown blends -

so, it made her quite furious . . .

When those dirty, pesky insects tried hitching a ride

On her long beautiful ears or her tender backside.

So furious, in fact, she *never* resented the tub

Where Annie lathered her gently and would carefully scrub.

She desired a fine coat no matter what it would take.

And always thanked her sweet Annie ...with a showering shake!

But all was not sunshine in Francesca's charmed life.

For there was something she craved, and it gave her great strife.

Weeks upon weeks, it corroded her mind,

And there seemed no solution - no obvious kind.

What could possibly be remiss for this one special dog,

Who received more kisses than the fairy tale frog?

ll, a curious discovery revealed what was lacking.
utside, wagged a friendly beast, filthy and hacking!

And though **scary** and **icky** this curious sight,

Gave her **warm** loving feelings night after long night.

Until the day she and Annie
walked side-by-bike to the park,
Where Fran's toys lay buried
under sand, grass and bark.

When, lo and behold,
she spied 'the beast' in the trees!
Its fur muddy and matted
and harboring fleas.

Francesca sneered at the sight.
Yuck! Had she been insane?
But, Annie ran straight to him
with no sign of disdain.

Then Annie gasped, and whispered,

"You poor little thing!"

Seeing his shriveled hind legs

her tears started to sting.

She knew that those legs

 had never moved - not a wiggle

Then, the dog started kissing her,

 making her giggle!

Through happier tears, Annie snuggled this stray.
"We'll call you Lucky," she managed to say.
Lucky wagged, then barked, so desperate to play -
but jealous, Francesca growled and wandered away.

She found it amusing Annie called this dog "Lucky."
He was dirty and hungry — and he smelled *really* yucky.

Yet what puzzled her most
    and really challenged her mind
Was how he trotted on two legs -
    the others dragged behind.

They left scraggly lines where the dirt ran thick

She carefully placed Lucky
in the basket on her bike,

Brought him home, bathed him,
and fed him all he would like.

Francesca resented Lucky's bath
but she *really* had her fill
Of his cart, lovingly made,
   from *her* human's goodwill.

Annie had worked day and night,
   hammering nails into wood.
Then spent more hours making
   it as lovely as she could.

Then, Annie shrugged and said,

"Time to try this thing out!"

She placed Lucky inside it

and let out a shout:

"Go on you two!

Show me how friends can play!"

Lucky quickly took off,

swerving every which way!

In time, Lucky maneuvered

every tricky turn and jerk

With wheels crafted to replace

legs unable to work.

And Francesca grew certain,

beyond any slight doubt,

That she, too, needed a cart,

Annie *must* figure this out.

But the sweet lovely girl,

    unable to read her dog's mind,

Did not know Francesca's thoughts

    were so jealous and unkind.

Poor Annie thought her dog

settled near Lucky to bray

Because she loved him so dearly

or wanted to play.

Really, Francesca was puzzled:

could she be friends with a mutt?

But as she watched his love for Annie

she grew out of this rut.

She put a stop to her envy—

for this 'mutt' was really ...FUN!

And suddenly her soul became lighter

as if warmed by the sun!

And as Lucky got filthy,

Francesca gave it a whirl,

For both enjoyed time

with their favorite girl.

And bath time had become

an extra-sneaky fun treat

With two dogs in a bubbly tub

splashing Annie's bare feet.

Soon, those two were the very best of friends.

Once Francesca stopped resenting the cart on Lucky's end,

That rickety, worn cart

   made by Annie's loving hands,

Which often got stuck

   in the deep playground sands.

And when it did,

   Francesca would lend him a paw,

Then they would run side-by-side

   chasing after the ball

That was thrown by the girl,

   much, much wiser than she ...

Who understood

the deep value

In friendships of three.

The End

ABOUT THE AUTHOR

Sarah, age 4 with Heidi

Sarah Barnard was born and raised on the beautiful shores of Lake Michigan. She currently lives in Muskegon, Michigan with her husband, Steve, and their sweet rescued mutt, Maya – who's nearly as pampered as Francesca! Her early love of reading and creative writing paved the way for her to earn a Bachelor of Science degree in Elementary Education, and serve her well in her job as the media clerk at a local elementary library. In her off hours she is often creating images as a professional photographer. Sarah is thankful she and her siblings, Annie and Jay, were raised with silly basset hounds, like Francesca. She is also thankful for her husband, their three incredible daughters, and homemade chocolate chip cookies, for being there to help her through the hard times and celebrate the great times.

ABOUT THE ILLUSTRATOR

Kate, age 7 with Tinker

Katherine Bourdon is a native of West Michigan living in Muskegon. She taught vocal music in public and private schools in Michigan for more than 30 years and retired before pursuing her other passion in art. Katherine's artwork has received numerous awards throughout the years from exhibitions at the Krasl Art Center in St. Joseph, MI, the Muskegon Museum of Art, The Kalamazoo Institute of Arts and the Michigan Regional Arts Exhibition at the UICA in Grand Rapids. Her artwork has been purchased by private collectors in the Midwest and Canada, and has been acquired and displayed in several corporations, hotels and financial institutions throughout Michigan.

www.ingramcontent.com/pod-product-compliance
Lightning Source LLC
Chambersburg PA
CBHW061405160426
42811CB00114B/2388/J